The Great Sphinx Mystery

Martin Simon
Art by Andre Fernandes

Literacy Consultants
David Booth • Kathleen Corrigan

Contents

Chapter 1

Visiting the Sphinx

Sophia and her little brother, Matt, were visiting their Uncle Mike in Egypt. Uncle Mike was an archaeologist. The kids were excited. Uncle Mike had taken them to see the Great Sphinx.

"Wow! It's huge!" Matt yelled as they drew near the Sphinx. "And look at all the people here!"

"Why are there so many people here today, Uncle Mike?" asked Sophia.

"Today is Labor Day in Egypt," replied Uncle Mike. "It's a holiday, so most people don't work. That's why there are more people at the Sphinx. Come on, let's walk to my tent for a cold drink."

As they walked, Sophia and Matt saw many people selling souvenirs.

"Hi, Mr. Mike!" shouted one vendor.

"Oh hi, Ali," said Uncle Mike. "Meet Sophia and Matt."

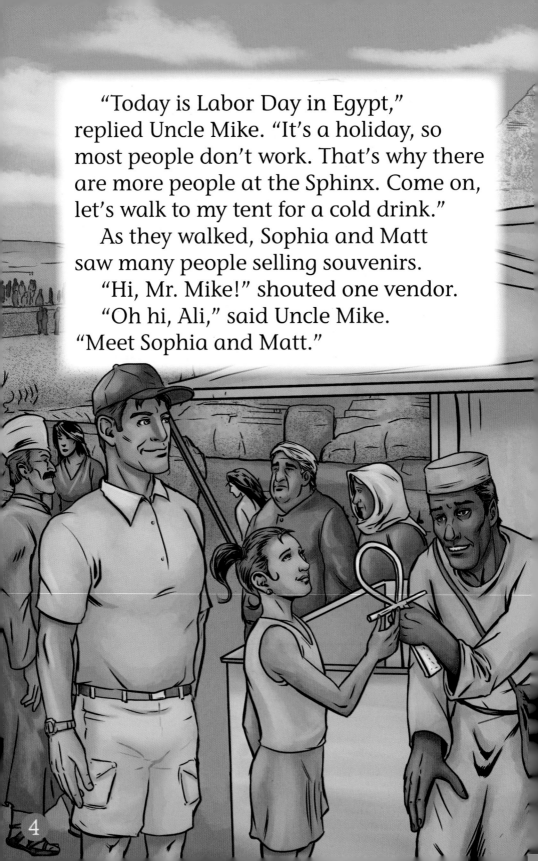

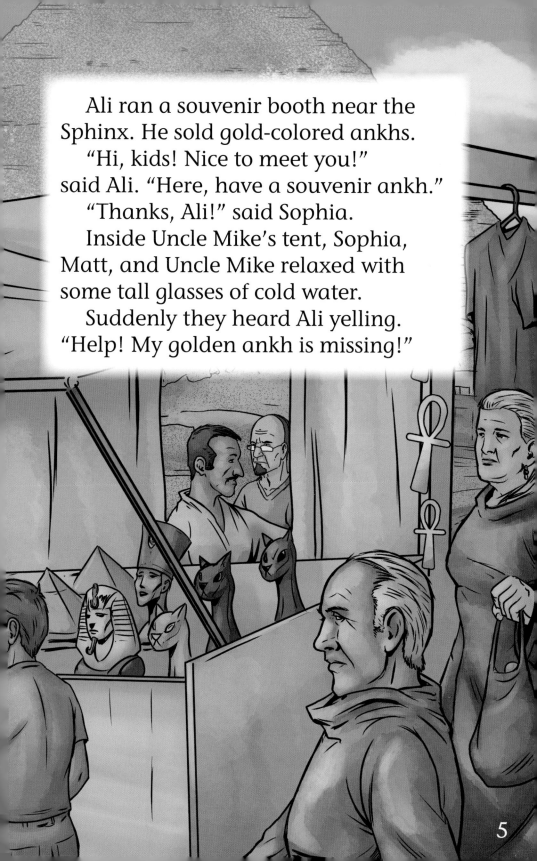

Ali ran a souvenir booth near the Sphinx. He sold gold-colored ankhs.

"Hi, kids! Nice to meet you!" said Ali. "Here, have a souvenir ankh."

"Thanks, Ali!" said Sophia.

Inside Uncle Mike's tent, Sophia, Matt, and Uncle Mike relaxed with some tall glasses of cold water.

Suddenly they heard Ali yelling. "Help! My golden ankh is missing!"

Chapter 2

Sophia and Matt Are on the Case!

Everyone rushed outside. Ali was at his booth, looking very upset.

"My special ankh is gone!" said Ali. "It's real gold! This ankh has been in my family for many years. I cannot lose it! Who could have taken it?"

"Don't worry, Ali," said Matt. "We can help you find it."

"What happened?" asked Uncle Mike.

"I went to take my afternoon nap in my hammock. I hung my gold ankh on the tent pole, as I always do. My ankh looks like the fake gold ankhs I sell. So I never worried about it being stolen."

"Does anyone know that your ankh is made of real gold?" asked Matt.

"Only three of my friends," said Ali. "I showed it to Dr. Jones, the head archaeologist. I also showed it to Omar. He sells souvenirs in the booth next to mine. The last person is Sara. She's Dr. Jones's student. But they are my friends. I don't believe that any of them would have stolen it."

"But they're our only suspects. We should talk to them," said Sophia.

Chapter 3

The Three Suspects

Uncle Mike led the kids to Dr. Jones. He was shocked when he heard that Ali's gold ankh had disappeared.

"That's terrible! Poor Ali. That ankh is so important to him," said Dr. Jones.

"What were you doing this afternoon, Dr. Jones?" asked Matt.

"I was learning to draw Egyptian symbols," replied Dr. Jones. "Want to see some of my work?"

Dr. Jones showed them the papers lying on his desk. They were covered with symbols. Matt noticed that the ink was not even dry on many of the sheets.

"Those are beautiful," said Sophia. "We'll let you know if we hear anything about the missing ankh."

Next, the children headed to Omar's tent. He sold Sphinx statues in a booth next to Ali's.

"I feel sorry for Ali," said Omar when he heard about the missing gold ankh. "I have been busy all day making cakes for Labor Day. I didn't notice anyone near Ali's booth during his nap."

The children noticed that Omar's arms were covered in flour. They looked around Omar's tent. The table was covered with pots and pans. They smelled cakes baking in the oven.

"Thanks, Omar!" said Sophia. "We'll let you know if we hear anything about the missing ankh."

Outside the tent, Matt said, "Let's go see Sara. She's Dr. Jones's student."

When they got there, Sara was working at a desk in her tent. The children told her about Ali's missing ankh. Sara looked worried.

"How's Ali?" she asked.

"Ali's really sad," replied Sophia. "The ankh has been in his family for years. His family really treasures it."

"Oh dear. Poor Ali," said Sara.

"What were you doing this afternoon, Sara?" asked Matt.

"Oh," said Sara. "I was busy with some Egyptian workers. We were clearing sand away from the Sphinx."

The two kids looked at each other.

"Thank you, Sara," Sophia said as they left.

"Quick, Matt! Let's find Ali! I know who did it!"

Uncle Mike asked Dr. Jones, Omar, and Sara to meet at Ali's booth.

"Ali, we know who took your gold ankh!" announced Sophia. "Sara, you owe Ali an apology. He has been very upset since you stole his gold ankh."

Chapter 4

Mystery Solved!

Sara turned red. "H–How did you know it was me?" she stammered.

"You said you were at the Sphinx with workers today," said Sophia.

"But today is a holiday," added Matt. "They were not at work! So your story can't be true!"

Sara pulled the gold ankh out from behind her and handed it to Ali.

"How could you, Sara?" asked Ali.

"I'm sorry, Ali," said Sara. "I needed money for my trip home. Forgive me?"

"I forgive you," said Ali. "But stealing is no way to solve problems!"

"Sara should help out at Ali's booth for a month to make it up to him," said Dr. Jones. Sara nodded in agreement.

"That's fair," replied Ali. "Thank you, Sophia and Matt. I'm glad that you were both working on Labor Day!"